D1443607

Scavengers:
Eating Nature's Trash

Opossums

Emma Carlson Berne

PowerKiDS
press

New York

Published in 2015 by The Rosen Publishing Group, Inc.
29 East 21st Street, New York, NY 10010

First Edition

Editor: Joanne Randolph
Book Design: Joe Carney
Photo Research: Katie Stryker

Photo Credits: Cover Ivan Kuzmin/Shutterstock.com; pp. 5, 9 erniedecker/iStock/Thinkstock; p. 7 Roy Toft/National Geographic/Getty Images; p. 8 Elliotte Rusty Harold/Shutterstock.com; p. 10 rthoma/Shutterstock.com; p. 11 monkeystock/iStock/Thinkstock; p. 12 ivkuzmin/iStock/Thinkstock; p. 13 Brock Meeler/iStock/Thinkstock; p. 15 Craig Hosterman/Shutterstock.com; p. 16 Phillip W. Kirkland/Shutterstock.com; p. 17 Karine Aigner/National Geographic/Getty Images; p. 18 Cathy Clark aka CLCsPics/Flickr/Getty Images; p. 19 Stacy Barnett/iStock/Thinkstock; p. 20 David Arango/iStock/Thinkstock; p. 21 James Hager/Robert Harding World Imagery/Getty Images; p. 22 JLFCapture/E+/Getty Images.

Library of Congress Cataloging-in-Publication Data

Berne, Emma Carlson, author.
 Opossums / by Emma Carlson Berne. — First edition.
     pages cm. — (Scavengers: eating nature's trash)
 Includes index.
 ISBN 978-1-4777-6602-6 (library binding) — ISBN 978-1-4777-6603-3 (pbk.) — ISBN 978-1-4777-6604-0 (6-pack)
 1. Opossums—Juvenile literature. 2. Scavengers (Zoology)—Juvenile literature. 3. Ecology—Juvenile literature. I. Title.
 QL737.M34B47 2015
 599.2'76—dc23
                                    2013050437

Manufactured in the United States of America

CPSIA Compliance Information: Batch #WS14PK6: For Further Information contact Rosen Publishing, New York, New York at 1-800-237-9932

Contents

Picture an opossum. Are you picturing a gray creature that looks like a very large rat? Perhaps you have seen one crouching near your knocked-over garbage cans.

People are used to thinking of opossums as dirty and disgusting. These **scavengers** are actually quiet, gentle animals that do not harm people or carry dangerous diseases. They eat insect pests and dead animals that would otherwise pollute our earth. Like all animals, the opossum is an important, useful member of our ecosystem.

Amazing Defense

Opossums are almost totally immune to the venom from rattlesnakes, cottonmouths, and other poisonous snakes.

Possums tend to have gray fur, with darker and lighter parts. They have pointed snouts, with pink noses, and round ears and small eyes that are set close together on their faces.

Native Animals

Opossums are **native** to North America, Central America, and South America. Early settlers from Europe had never seen opossums before. One wrote that the opossum looked like a "monkey fox." Other people have called it a bush rat and a forest rat.

Where Virginia Opossums Live

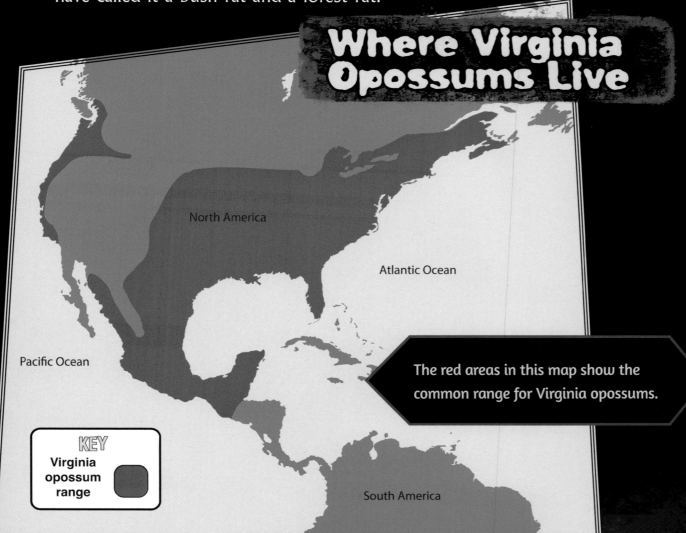

North America

Atlantic Ocean

Pacific Ocean

The red areas in this map show the common range for Virginia opossums.

KEY
Virginia opossum range

South America

This is *Didelphis marsupialis*, also called the common opossum. It lives throughout Central and South America. Like the Virginia opossum, this opossum can climb trees and will eat whatever is available.

In North America, the **nocturnal** opossum lives in the eastern, midwestern, and southern states. Opossums try to avoid cold weather, so they don't inhabit the northernmost parts of the United States or Canada. There are two **species** found in North America. One kind is called *Didelphis virginiana*, the Virginia opossum. This is the kind you are probably used to seeing. The other species is mainly found in Mexico. It is called

Where Are the Opossums?

Unlike many animals, opossums don't have a specific **territory**. Instead, they wander from place to place, **foraging** for food. They prefer to live near woods and near water. They like small streams best so that they can fish. Woods provide lots of hollow trees for **dens**. They also have plenty of nuts, berries, and insects, which are all things opossums like to eat.

Opossums like to live in forests, where they can climb trees for safety. Much of the food they like to eat can also be found in forests.

Opossums live near people, too. They are happy to eat garbage and pet food left outside by people.

Opossums like to live near fields of crops, too, so they can eat the grain and insects there. Often, opossums will nest in the abandoned burrows of other animals, piles of brush, or in barns, sheds, or attics.

Our Only Marsupial

Even though they are much bigger, opossums resemble large rats. They have pointy faces and long, naked tails. They have long, gray fur and big, black eyes, with excellent nighttime vision.

Here you can see how this baby opossum's hands look like a human's. You can also see its pointy snout. Opossums have a lot of teeth packed into their narrow jaws.

Opossums can curl their semiprehensile tails around branches to help them climb safely.

Opossums use their **semiprehensile** tails to grip tree branches when they climb to keep them from falling. Adult opossums cannot hang by their tails, as their tails are not strong enough. They have flexible paws that look almost like human hands. These paws are good for gripping as the opossum climbs trees. Opossums are also North America's only **marsupials**. Marsupial females have pouches in their bellies for carrying and nursing their babies. Kangaroos are marsupials, too.

To Be Roadkill or to Eat Roadkill?

Opossums will eat all sorts of scavenged food, including dead animals, discarded human food scraps, pet food, and livestock feed. They need a lot of calcium, so they eat the skeletons of the **carrion** they consume.

This opossum found a nice dead rodent to eat. It has carried the dead animal up into a tree so it can eat safely.

This opossum has walked onto the road to see if it can find any food. If a car comes at the wrong time, the opossum could end up as a meal for the next scavenger.

Their diet is the reason we often see opossums lying dead by the side of the highway. Opossums venture out by the road to eat other animals killed by cars. Cars frighten the opossums, though. Unfortunately for the opossums, they have a unique defense when they are scared. They will lie down and play dead. When they do this on a road, this often means cars will hit them.

Opossums Eat Everything!

There's not a lot opossums won't eat. They are **omnivores** and eat fruit, berries, frogs, snails, worms, corn, grains of all kinds, fish, crayfish, grass, and all kinds of plants. Opossums aren't very good hunters, though. Instead of chasing down and killing small **prey**, they prefer insects, like grasshoppers, beetles, and ants.

Dead rabbits and dead chickens are a particular favorite, but they will eat just about any dead or rotten creature. Opossums like to eat small mice, shrews, and birds, too. These animals have to be already dead, sick, or injured for the opossums to get them, though.

Pet food that has been left outside makes an easy meal for an opossum.

Swimmers and Climbers

Opossums are very good tree climbers, partly due to their wonderful, sensitive tails. Baby opossums can even hang upside down from tree branches by their tails. Opossums can use their tails as a sort of fifth hand. They sometimes hold their tails in a loop and use the loop to hold dry leaves or other nest material.

Opossums can climb fences, as this one is doing.

This opossum has climbed to the top of a tree.

The opossum moves slowly in a kind of swaying walk. It can run, though, up to about 4 miles per hour (6 km/h). Opossums are good swimmers and can even swim totally underwater. Opossums sometimes stroll around in shallow water, as if they are simply enjoying it.

Playing Possum

Opossums are not **aggressive** animals. In fact, when confronted with a **predator**, they will usually run away and try to climb up a tree. When faced with danger, though, opossums also lie down, hold perfectly still, and even open their mouths so that they look like dead animals. Their heart rate and breathing slow way down. The opossum might stay like this for hours or for only a few minutes.

Opossums do not only stiffen their bodies and close their eyes to appear dead. They also give off a foul smell from glands on their bodies to help sell their act even more.

Opossums that are playing dead will continue their act even if they are picked up and carried away. Once they feel sure the coast is clear, they will loosen their muscles and be on their way.

If an opossum is faced with another threatening opossum, it might stop, open its mouth, show its teeth, and hiss. At this warning, the other opossum might leave

Life as a Baby Opossum

For most of their lives, opossums live alone. The adult males and females meet only to mate in the winter and early summer. The mother opossum is pregnant for only 13 days. When the babies are born, they are just the size of honeybees.

For the first couple months after the baby opossums are born, they stay in their mother's pouch and nurse.

Baby opossums are known for hitching a ride on their mother's back as she goes in search of food.

The baby opossums crawl straight into their mother's pouch. They stay in the pouch, nursing continuously, for almost two months. Then, when they are about 70 days old, the babies climb out of the pouch. They follow their mother, learning to climb and forage for food by watching her. They ride on her back when she goes off to search for food. When they are tired, they climb back in the pouch.

Opossums and People

Many people think of opossums as dirty annoyances. In fact, opossums are immune to many diseases. They are less likely to carry rabies than wild dogs or raccoons.

Though they might occasionally rummage through your trash can, they are shy and not aggressive. They help clean up the dead animals that can make humans sick. In fact, next time you see an opossum in your yard, consider welcoming it instead of chasing it off.

Opossums are helpful to humans in their job as scavengers.

Glossary

aggressive (uh-GREH-siv) Ready to fight.

carrion (KAR-ee-un) Dead, rotting flesh.

dens (DENZ) Wild animals' homes.

foraging (FOR-ij-ing) Hunting or searching for something.

marsupials (mahr-SOO-pee-ulz) Types of animals that carry their young in pouches.

native (NAY-tiv) Born or grown in a certain place or country.

nocturnal (nok-TUR-nul) Active during the night.

omnivores (OM-nih-vorz) Animals that eat both plants and animals.

predator (PREH-duh-ter) An animal that kills other animals for food.

prey (PRAY) An animal that is hunted by another animal for food.

scavengers (SKA-ven-jurz) Animals that eat dead things.

semiprehensile (seh-mee-pree-HENT-sul) Able to help in climbing or to let an animal hang from a branch.

species (SPEE-sheez) One kind of living thing. All people are one species.

territory (TER-uh-tor-ee) Land or space that animals guard for their use.

Websites

Due to the changing nature of Internet links, PowerKids Press has developed an online list of websites related to the subject of this bo This site is updated regularly. Please use this link to access the list:
www.powerkidslinks.com/scav/oposs/